1:100 LEADERSHIP SOLUTION

A PRACTICAL GUIDE TO HELP YOU BE THE LEADER YOU WOULD WANT

By Daryl D. Black

For more content, including bonus material like
the 1:100 Leadership Solution

For resources be sure to go to:

www.daryldblack.com

ISBN #9781775283003

"When we are no longer able to change a situation,
we are challenged to change ourselves."
— Viktor E. Frankl, Man's Search for Meaning

To my dude, Hunter.

You're my 'Why'.

I can't say I'm the perfect Dad. Some days I win, many days I lose.

But I can say that I bring it each and every day just like I hope you will continue to do.

That's all anyone can ask of another.

Contents

INTRODUCTION

Leadership is difficult.

Have you ever wondered where to start when it comes to developing or improving your leadership skills? How to connect with those around you? Don't worry, you aren't alone.

In leadership we are dealing with some of the most complex elements in the world: human beings. The complexities that make up how we think, feel and act are seemingly infinite when viewed singularly. Now put many individuals together in a team and the variables that drive behaviour increase exponentially. To add to that we are dealing with our internal biases, emotions and norms.

In the light of this we don't need more theoretical leadership advice.

The good news is that leadership is a set of skills and behaviours; skills and behaviours that can be learned through mindful observation, dedicated reflection, obtaining knowledge, practice, feedback and continual refinement.

Go to any local bookstore or surf online and you'll be bombarded with hundreds of books containing hundreds of pages of advice backed by the latest studies. While well-meaning and valuable, these books and myriad concepts won't help in the 'heat of the moment' that is characteristic of crisis especially. From personal experience, I can say that we don't need a bookshelf of books and hundreds of pages of words. Particularly during a crisis, the context by which we'll discuss leadership, we need a point of reference, so we can effectively connect with individuals and teams, sometimes remotely. Further, this reference needs to be straightforward, actionable and sustainable. Oh, as if that weren't hard enough, the reference needs to be applicable in a stressful, time-constrained, information-deficient environment.

LEAD YOURSELF FIRST

The solution to this cacophony of requirements revolves around the concept that only when we control what happens on the inside can we effectively influence what happens on the outside. To put it another way, we need to ensure that our stress levels, emotions and internal dialogue are in check before we can hope to connect with and lead others around us. Once we have built the personal connections then we can move toward a goal or solution.

"Leadership during crisis requires you to look inward first. Only when you can master what happens on the inside can you influence what happens on the outside."

Daryl D. Black

@daryldblack

LEADERSHIP CLIMATE: WHAT WE SAY MATTERS

Whether we recognize it or not, as leaders, we are either building or detracting from our ability to connect with and lead others. To that end:

WHAT we say matters;
HOW we say it matters;
HOW we act matters.

How a team interacts & communicates with you as the leader is not a reflection on them.

It is direct reflection on how you interact and communicate with them.

Daryl D. Black

www.daryldblack.com

We need to recognize that **we** create an environment around us, a mood, that directly and profoundly influences how those around us talk to us, act around us and trust us. Think about Darth Vader. Yes, a fictional character but it illustrates the point really well. How did Darth Vader treat the team? What mood did the 'team' have when they were around him? Was there reluctance to give him bad news because the reaction would be really negative and the consequences severe?

To gauge your own leadership climate as we call it, ask yourself whether your team brings you 'bad news' openly and in a timely fashion? It's an important question because we rarely run into challenges with someone giving us good news so that doesn't tell us as much as conveying something unfavourable does. If the answer is no to 'bad news' then that could be a symptom of a climate that doesn't promote clear exchange of information and team safety. If you answered yes then don't put this book down, there is a lot more we can dive into that will really take the connections to the next level.

With all of that said, this is my answer to the challenges of leadership, particularly during crisis.

It's my *1:100 Leadership Solution* and it starts with this question:

TODAY, WAS I THE LEADER I WOULD WANT?

The intent of this solution is to be simple, actionable and straightforward. It has a direct relationship with lead yourself first. To break it down a bit further, the Solution is broken into Four Personal Pillars of Effective Leadership:

1. Vulnerability,
2. Empathy,
3. Compassion and
4. Personal stress management.

To be clear, the deeper you go to answer this, the deeper the impact.

THE ORIGIN OF THE 1:100 LEADERSHIP SOLUTION

The 1:100 Leadership Solution is the result of my own challenges in leadership, particularly during a crisis. These challenges range from how to handle my own stress levels, communicate effectively with others, create a high-performing team rapidly, motivate the team and ensure that the team is doing what it needs to do to solve problems. The list of challenges is long and almost impossible to grapple with when viewed together. Almost I said.

I have experienced a lot of chaos in my life, in particular my 27 years in search and rescue and emergency management. During all of those years, I have dealt (and continue to deal with) hundreds, if not thousands of people suffering. I've seen this because I belong to teams that respond to and manage emergencies ranging from a relatively small search and rescue operation to Katrina and the like. In fact, I have the distinction of being in the Emergency Operations Centre (disaster response headquarters) on two of Canada's largest natural disasters. These environments are not for the faint of heart. The decisions are made at breakneck speed, with little to no information (and the information you do have is likely incorrect at worse or incomplete at best). The consequences of your actions can impact hundreds or thousands of people and stress levels are extremely high among the team. The team is often comprised of all manners of individuals from a trained responder to an administration clerk. It is a chaotic and dynamic environment and not easily explained unless you've seen or been a part of it.

Through the years, I developed a ritual that kept me focused on my role as an effective leader while ensuring that I continued to improve, even incrementally. It made my leadership journey much more deliberate. It served me very well during both professional and personal situations, especially when facing crisis.

At the end of each day (or night), I'd ask myself: Today, was I the leader I would want? Yes, that's it. There are no mantras, no acronyms, no secret meanings. I would go through the various interactions I had that day with my peers, the team and others I encountered, either in direct conversation, email or whatever means that applied. I would intentionally think about my words (if I remembered them), my body language, how others may have perceived me and how various people interacted with me.

When I first started asking myself the question and replaying my days, the filter was very broad. Basically, did we get the job done? Was I a nice guy? Yes, in that order. Over time, I realized that I was using more specific criteria because I determined these to be the most effective for leadership, connecting with individuals and, as it turns out, closest to my values. Those were *vulnerability, compassion, empathy* and *managing my personal stress levels.* I would determine where I ineffectively demonstrated, say, vulnerability, and I would be more conscious of it during the next shift. Each time I found myself in a leadership position, I enacted the ritual of asking whether I was the leader I would want to the point of putting it into my smartphone to remind me at the end of each day.

Because I find it so effective for me *personally* and colleagues when I explain it to them, I decided that it was time to further refine and make it more widely available. It is a deceptively simple solution and my intent has always been to use something that isn't overly complicated.

I am still a practitioner of leadership, I enact the Solution and have since replaced the word 'leader' with 'parent', 'partner', 'coach'…you get the idea.

In principle the 1:100 Leadership Solution is:

- Easy to learn.
- Easy to do.
- It can be as complex or simple as you want.
- Rooted in complex and proven concepts.
- Leads to a depth not realized by other techniques.

The technique is deceptively simple but don't be fooled. It will lead to improvements around stress management, communication, decision-making, team building and much more.

SO WHY 1%? SHOULDNT WE STRIVE FOR 100%?

The premise is that if we improve even 1% each day, then we are moving in the right direction. We are being conscious and deliberate in improving and leaving less to chance. Leadership isn't static. We are either improving our leadership or detracting from it. Period. Like compound interest, incremental and constant improvement leads to exponential gain. If each day brings us just 1% closer to 100%, then we are making progress.

Would we like 100%? Of course. Is it realistic? No. Leadership is hard. We are dealing with the most complex of variables: human beings. One on one interactions are a dance between two people. Anyone who has been in a relationship recognizes that. Now add MULTIPLE people to that mix and you get an incredible combination of personalities and complexities. The 1:100 Leadership Solution gives us a means to connect with individuals effectively, which in turn greatly improves team performance and outcomes.

"Leadership is not one grandiose gesture.
Nor is it a certificate on the wall, a
higher salary or a gold name plate on the desk.

Rather it is the **accumulation** of
encouraging **words**, positive **actions**,
effective **decisions** and meaningful
personal **connections** made over time."

Daryl D. Black

www.daryldblack.com

PERSONAL AND PROFESSIONAL CRISIS AS THE CONTEXT

Crisis is defined as a time of great difficulty, intense danger, or when important decisions need to be made. It is an area I am particularly used to as I have encountered personal and professional crises like all of you. *The characteristics of crisis apply regardless if the crisis is personal or professional.* Examples of symptoms of both personal and professional crisis are increased stress, information may be inadequate, and time is often a factor among hundreds of others. Think about the last time you experienced personal crisis. Maybe it was a job loss, death in the family, a divorce. I would suspect that you felt stress, that you didn't have all the information you wanted to feel comfortable to make a decision and as much as we would have liked to crawl under a rock and let the world go by (or by contrast leap into solving the problems) practical matters needed to be dealt with.
If we can lead during crisis, then in 'non-crisis' situations we'll do just fine. To be clear, I'm not encouraging you to intentionally seek out crisis , but we all face it. We may as well learn to lead through it.

Most importantly, crisis leads to breakthroughs.

ABOUT THIS GUIDE

Above all, this guide is meant to be practical and straightforward.

Most of the content is a compendium of blog posts I've written with additional content and context added.

The beginning is the list of questions that make up the 1:100 Leadership Solution. The 1% means that you don't have to go through each sub-question. In the spirit of incremental improvement, leading to profound change starts with only one or two sub-questions.

Following the 1:100 Leadership Solution are various sections relevant to the Personal Pillars in particular. These sections are meant to provide additional background and perspective so that you may further understand what that concept is about and why it is important.

We must recognize that improvement doesn't happen in one grandiose, sweeping gesture or a particular moment. Improvement happens through consistent and small actions. Like exercising, we don't see the gains (or losses if that's what you want!) the next morning. Over time and with sustained and consistent actions, we can see great aggregate results. In a relationship, your feelings aren't defined by that ONE moment. It's through the consistent expression of feelings, the seemingly small gestures, yes, the occasional big actions that lead to a relationship.

The incremental improvement applies to leadership, especially during crisis where we need to be even more specific and effective in improving. Each day, we are either contributing to or detracting from our leadership. It's that simple.

To help you get started and to be more deliberate in implementing the 1:100 Leadership Solution you'll find a journal of sorts in the section called the 60-Day Daily Improvement Routine, which includes daily questions for each of the 60 days.

THIS IS MY EXPERIENCE

I don't have a lot of letters after my name (see additional guidance for my thoughts on that topic) nor does my vocation end in "-ologist".

This book contains ideas, concepts and techniques that I personally use, and lessons learned from seeing people at their very best and very worst. My textbook is not from the classroom or field trips. It is written on the fly, mostly during crisis. As I wrote above, crisis is a Petri dish where all the variables and factors of human behavior are thrown in where they can be more easily observed and the effects of said behaviours amplified greatly.

IT'S A BUFFET APPROACH

Let's face it: I'm not you. Yes, surprising I know. That means what works well for me works because it closely aligns with my personal values and approach to dealing with people. What follows is not meant to be an overly-prescriptive set of rules. Every person is different, every situation is different. Literally. Treat this book as a guide; a collection of principles. The 1:100 Leadership Solution gives you a place to start and is meant to give you something to be more deliberate and conscious in how you lead yourself and in turn, others.

Some things will resonate, others won't. That's okay, expected and encouraged. If something doesn't sound right then it means that you've taken some time already to think about who you are, how you choose to interact with others. If that's the case, then you're already off to a great start.

To continue the journey, check out a link to my other content at daryldblack.com.

THE 1:100 LEADERSHIP SOLUTION

THE QUESTION:

1. Daily, ask yourself: "Today, was I the leader I would've wanted?"

2. If the answer is no, then "How could I improve?"

3. Improve.

   1% each day is a big deal.

The 1:100 Leadership Solution

How To Be the Leader You Would Want

During crisis:

1. Daily, ask yourself:
   "**Today, was I the leader I would've wanted**?"

2. If the answer is no: "**How can I improve**?"

3. **Improve**.

1% each day is a big deal.

Daryl D. Black

www.daryldblack.com

VULNERABILITY

o   Did I say, "I don't necessarily have all the answers"?
o   Did I ask for help?
o   Did I take ownership and accountability for a situation or decision that happened?

EMPATHY

o   Did I intentionally see a situation from a team member's perspective?
o   Did I regularly ask team members, "How are you doing?" and genuinely CARE about the answer?
o   Did I take the time to actively listen, to be truly present in a conversation with a team member?

COMPASSION

- o Did I stop beating myself up for a decision or action taken?
- o Did I show kindness to a team member?
- o Did I support a team member who made a mistake?

PERSONAL STRESS MANAGEMENT

- o Did I recognize moments of self-stress? When and why?
- o Did I take steps to mitigate my stress proactively?
- o Did I recognize self-stress and act accordingly to deal with it?

PILLAR #1: VULNERABILITY

- Did I say, "I don't necessarily have all the answers"?

  - Did I ask for help?

- Did I take ownership and accountability for a situation or decision that happened?

The 1:100 Leadership Solution

Personal Pillar of Effective Leadership # 1

Vulnerability

- Did I say: **"I don't have all the answers"**?

- Did I ask for **help**?

- Did I openly take **ownership** and **accountability**
  for a situation or decision?

Daryl D. Black

www.daryldblack.com

VULNERABILITY – WHY IT MATTERS

So, what is vulnerability and why is it discussed in a leadership book about crisis leadership? Not the physical kind of vulnerability either (walking on a tightrope or running rapids without a life jacket). I guess it means different things for different people. It could be speaking in front of a crowd. It could be planning without the full picture. For others, maybe it's leaving one job for another. Maybe it's asking for assistance with a project. For me, it's the potential sharing of my inner self, especially when stress levels are high, which is common during crisis. For example, writing a blog and letting others see it! I have come to realize to a certain extent vulnerability is critical to personal growth, meaningful relationships and leadership. We'll discuss the criticality of vulnerability relative to leadership shortly.

I've been an instructor for many years and I remember one of the maxims. If a student asks you a question that you don't know the answer to, then don't be afraid to say, 'I don't know...but I'll get you the answer.' I suppose that's an indication of vulnerability in a very superficial sense. That said, I know that my first instinct is to come up with an answer.

One of my favourite authors, Brene Brown (*Daring Greatly*, a must read) and TED Talkers (ted.com), started me down this path. As I went down the path of introspection and the notion of vulnerability, particularly as it pertains to leadership, so many things that she said resonated with me. I actually think that vulnerability is a critical trait in ourselves and bringing people together and supporting one another. Yet, it is often overlooked in leadership conversations. Until now.

WHY SHOULD WE SHOW VULNERABILITY ANYWAY?!

Trust:
Trust is really the foundational element, a very basic element, in building meaningful relationships (personal, business, parental etc.).   As human beings, we are hardwired to fear the unknown. It goes back to our Caveman days. Humans HAD to be skeptical and fearful and frankly, pessimistic. To ensure the survival of humanity I NEEDED my quest for fire/wheel-building ancestors to worry every minute of every day about what they would eat and how they'd survive!! A virtual tip of the hat to them by the way. Job well done. You got us this far. Thank you. If you reveal something about yourself ("This is a difficult situation and I don't have all the answers"), something that others may not know, then it is one less unknown for instance.

There is also another advantage to being vulnerable; it creates trust. In the RIGHT SETTING, opening up tells others that you trust THEM. You trust them enough to open up. To be honest and transparent. Depending on the SETTING, it is exactly what is needed because it is an overt display that I TRUST you enough to open myself up.

SENSE OF "THEYRE NOT INFALLIBLE. THEYRE LIKE ME"

Similar to the above, we as humans are hardwired to belong to a group. Some call it a tribe, teams, collective, etc. From an evolutionary perspective, we don't possess the physical prowess and tools to have survived on our own. We had to divide up labour, hunt in packs and use each other's strengths to serve the greater good, otherwise NO ONE would've survived. To belong to a group, we'd have to have something, usually many things, in common. Well, our needs have changed, and the threats are no longer sabre-tooth tigers wanting to eat us but that hardwired need to belong is inherent in us. You just need to look at how you view a 'rival' city and its sports team. They aren't 'US.'

Which relates back to vulnerability. If I KNOW you feel like me, view things like me, or are willing to express something internal to me, then I will feel a connection. It's not BS, it's nature.

Remember that vulnerability builds trust and trust is essential for team-building.

Vulnerability is not weakness. It is the opposite, so we need to get over it. It's really a simple equation: As a leader, I show vulnerability and I get something in return: trust. Trust is the key to cohesion and connection. On the surface, it seems like showing 'weakness' would erode the bond between a leader and follower but it is the exact opposite. To be clear, like so many things, vulnerability must be used in moderation, otherwise the team will lose confidence because the 'Boss' isn't cut out for this.

Just so we're clear. There is a time and place for showing vulnerability. In the world of crisis, an area I'm pretty well-versed in, there is ABSOLUTELY a need to be strong, stoic, and steadfast. It is not, it not a time to show vulnerability. When deployed to manage a crisis, such as the flood of 2013 in Calgary and High River, or The Beast in 2016, the wildfire that decimated Ft. McMurray, strength is imperative. We must make hundreds or thousands of significant decisions, and there is little time to reveal yourself or your inner turmoil. To be part of an extremely well-performing team, each member has had to reveal a part of themselves in order to really gain the trust of his/her teammates (more on that later). I trust those teammates, and I mean this quite literally, with my life. And they trust me with theirs.

SO, WHY DON'T WE?!

I can only speak for myself of course. Maybe it applies to others, maybe it doesn't. For me, it's the fact that I don't know if we're there yet. I don't show vulnerability to my parents. I don't want them to worry. I don't really show it to my brother. I gauge carefully before showing it to a new team to determine time and place. I struggle to show it in personal relationships.

Frankly, I don't want to ALWAYS be invincible...the pillar. Of course, it's a role I can fill and do quite well and with minimal drama. But once the crisis is over, I WANT to be able to let my guard down. I NEED to. The facade I put up can only last so long. Sometimes, it's hours, days, or weeks but eventually something must give. It's imperative and healthy in fact. For me to be authentic, I want to put the persona of 'tough guy, Alpha male' away and just FEEL. Yes, FEEL. I sometimes don't even know what that means. Sometimes it's pride, sometimes it's pain, sometimes it's absolute exhaustion, and sometimes it's profound sadness. It doesn't matter nor should it.

IF ALL YOU HAVE IS A HAMMER

As a culture, as a society, we need to recognize that the Depression is done, the World Wars have been fought, the great physical demands of building railroads are gone, and our society has evolved to have far more complex problems where physical strength, intimidation and brute force are no longer the best or only option. The adage rings true: If all you have is a hammer, then every problem is a nail. There are an infinite number of variables at play these days. A micro version of this is when my nine-year-old dude has a problem with a kid at the playground. The old-school mentality would be to kick the other kid's ass. Oh, yes that is ALWAYS an option and yes, maybe the ultimate solution, but I want my son to be able to try some other things before the punch to the nose. What has he done to contribute to the situation?

THE ORIGINS OF THE 'STRONG' LEADER AND 'BE A MAN' PARADIGM

I'll explore crisis leadership and this paradigm that a leader needs to be 'strong'. In macho terms, the leader needs to 'Be a man.' I am building on the discussion about Vulnerability and will 'walk the walk' by demonstrating it.

A quandary I have often faced is this notion around what it means to be a 'strong' leader and even how that is tied into the concept of 'Being a man.' So, I find myself pondering this question again and frequently. What does it mean to be a 'strong' leader' and more importantly, where do I fit in within that spectrum? It's a theme I've heard spoken throughout my life I now see. You just have to look for it. Sometimes it's overt while other times it is FAR more subversive...hidden and sinister. So, what are the expectations of a strong leader I find myself asking myself frequently? What is the 'typical' leader? What is the archetype? The Rock. Men don't cry. You're the man of the house. Don't be such a f#ckin' pussy. Men don't talk about their problems because we're men. Problem solvers. Hunters. Man up. Suck it up. Macho men are sexy. Strength is hot. Of course, I'm missing many more examples.

ARCHETYPE RECENT ORIGINS AND THE DOMINO EFFECT

Where does this come from? I'm no Freud. Heck, I need spellcheck to use the words 'sociology' and 'anthropology'. I'm just a guy doing the best he can. But I do have a curious (albeit inefficient) mind. The origins of this archetype likely go back hundreds, no, thousands of years and are still hardwired into us. I can only speak of the recent history, meaning since the 1900s as that's a history I have heard about directly from my own family and others.

THE GREAT WARS (WWI AND WWII)

During these incredibly tumultuous events, hundreds of thousands of men went to the front lines and fought while the women 'stayed back' or took on support roles. The surviving men returned home, suffering from shell shock (now called PTSD I'd suspect), sitting stoic and distant while the kids frolicked around with the mother telling the kids to be quiet or not to bother the father or grandpa for fear of upsetting whatever fragile equilibrium existed with the confines of the man's mind and psyche.

First domino pushed over.

THE GREAT DEPRESSION

This is another domino where thousands of families were decimated by a collapsed economy, famine and a host of other catastrophic cascading events. The stories of thousands of men lined up outside the factory gates waiting for a chance to work, even for a day, to provide for the family. Adults checking out the obituaries in the paper with the notion that with a death came a job opening. Men doing hours upon hours of labour and incredibly physically taxing jobs. This didn't just happen for six months, or even a year. It was a DECADE. 10 years!

Second domino pushed over.
Interspersed among those two all-reaching series of events are thousands of stories of our Grandads and Dads working the railroad or some other physically intensive endeavour (my Grandad and my dad for example but the railroad is just one example of where long and physical work was involved) where the value of hard work was lauded and preached. My paternal Grandad had a short, stocky build with thick fingers and solid shoulders. You don't get that from working as an accountant. Our dads went to work at a young age bringing back money into the family or helping the old man around the farm. Of course, during that time, formal education gave way to the need for the boys to forego schooling to help around the farm. I literally don't know what grade either of my Grandads got to but I'm damned sure it wasn't graduation from high school. For my paternal Grandad, I'm sure that circa-1950, CP Rail didn't have a fantastic education support plan.

The dominoes are in full motion.

So, the origins of a 'strong' leader and by association what it means to 'Be a man' historically means strong leaders and macho men have been strongly associated with each other. These dominoes were critical to the family unit and our society. That said, none of those elements required a lot, if any, connection to one's feelings much less the need to communicate any feelings to anyone else. The leader was strong, a pillar and had all the requisite behaviour (i.e. forcefulness, possible intimidation, hard charging approach to problem solving, lack of empathy and self-regulation) to continue to reinforce this paradigm.

So, what's changed? Why can't we continue along this path of a 'strong' leader?

MASLOWS HIERARCHY OF NEEDS

Today's problems are far more complex than those of the early 1900s. To be CRYSTAL clear, I am not saying that the Great War and Depression were not monumental problems. Those events jeopardized people's very survival. Maslow's Hierarchy of Needs states that there are multiple levels of needs. The aforementioned dominoes (Wars, Depression etc.) really dealt with the first two levels where literal survival was at stake. For those involved in the battles themselves, not just the soldiers, but the vast populations who were on the front-line, survival was not assured. For those not threatened physically, those of us in North America for instance, the 'bread winner', the pillar of the family was quite likely putting his life on the line, and the loss of that man would be catastrophic for families in terms of emotional (the foundation of our family is gone) and financial loss (remember that mothers weren't in the workforce so it's not like they could easily replace the income). I get it.

Fast forward to recent history where for the vast amount of the population, those two levels are now solved through economic and social programs, for example. I make no claim that we are universally safe but let's agree that most of us are taken care of as far as the first two levels are concerned. So that leaves us with the third level from the bottom and third from the top- Love and Belonging. Where do we get this satisfied? Where do we see this in modeled behaviour for what 'Be a Man' means? For most of us, it is in our parents.

Therein lies the rub. OUR parents are the products of THEIR upbringing. And who were they raised by? THEIR parents who were raised or raising families. You get the idea. The saying that when all you have is a hammer every problem is a nail rings true.

THE STRONG LEADER/BE A MAN PARADIGM NEEDS TO CHANGE

The definition of what it means to be a man needs to change because as a society, our collective needs have changed. We no longer need to worry about basic safety needs in the general sense. Yes, there are still those who do legitimately worry about their safety and basic needs. We need leaders that can grapple with more complex issues where the solution is not simply use brute force, intimidation, subversion or avoidance.

THE TAKEAWAY

Not only have society's needs changed but the needs of those immediately around us have: our partners, our kids, our teams, our organizations. Hell, even our parents have issues that they need help with (have you tried to teach your Dad how to attach a picture to an email?!)

I'm thinking there's not much debate there. Yeah, this isn't the Depression where we have to pray for a loaf of bread and water.

So, now that we've seen where we've come from, we need to figure out where to go and how we get there.

"**Vulnerability** isn't a measure of weakness. Rather, it's an essential ingredient of trust, which in turn, is an essential ingredient for leadership."

@daryldblack

CONFESSIONS OF A 'VULNERABLE' LEADER- MY OWN EXPERIENCE

Vulnerability is not weakness. It is the opposite, so we need to get over it. It's really a paradox in action. I show vulnerability and trust and vulnerability are returned to me.

Just so we're clear. **There is a time and place for showing vulnerability**. In the world of emergency response, an area I'm pretty well versed in, there is ABSOLUTELY a need to be strong, stoic, and steadfast. Strength is imperative. We are making significant decisions, and hundreds or thousands of them, and there is little time to be revealing yourself or your inner self. Now that said, to be part of an extremely well-performing team, each member of a high performing team has had to reveal a part of themselves to gain the trust of his/her teammates (more on that later). I trust those teammates, and I mean this quite literally, with my life. And they trust me with theirs.

Crisis hits us all and maybe that's not when we are on a deployment to the flood of 2013 in Calgary and High River or The Beast, the wildfire that decimated Ft. McMurray,

As a culture, as a society, we need to recognize that the Depression is done, the World Wars have been fought, the great physical demands of building railroads are gone and that our society has evolved to have far more complex problems where physical strength, intimidation and brute force are no longer the best or only option. The adage rings true: If all you have is a hammer, then every problem is a nail. There are an infinite number of variables at play these days. A micro version of this is when my 9-year-old dude has a problem with a kid at the playground. The old-school mentality would be to kick the other kids' ass. Oh, yes that is ALWAYS an option and yes, maybe the ultimate solution, but I want my son to be able to try some other things before the punch to the throat. For example, Dude, what have you done to contribute to the situation?

I had a situation on a deployment to a disaster scene. An individual took exception to something I did. I was in a position of authority over this person, he was in my section (a.k.a. department) and not someone I knew well. On his part it started with a rise from the table, stern words and a subsequent puffing of the chest (because that's what guys do). Instead of resorting to the usual, "I'm your boss so file in and shut up," I took a more sensible and humanist approach. I listened to his vent, I apologized, expressed vulnerability in that I was doing the best I could with little or no sleep and was pre-occupied with many other things. Further I asked for his help. He was a bit taken aback that the Alpha male would admit that he was tired and not his best self. As a result, he became an ally moving forward. If I had dropped the hammer right away, then he would've fallen into line but certainly not have supported me behind closed doors or would've done the bare minimum.

The point of that is that I'm being vulnerable in sharing that story as well as to illustrate that by being vulnerable myself, in that moment, I built a bridge with that individual

THE TAKEAWAY

Think about it. Vulnerability is not weakness. It's courage. Try it. Maybe even baby steps.

PILLAR #2:
EMPATHY

- Did I intentionally see a situation from a team member's perspective?

- Did I regularly ask team members, "How are you doing?" and genuinely CARE about the answer?

- Did I take the time to actively listen, to be truly present in a conversation with a team member?

The 1:100 Leadership Solution

Personal Pillar of Effective Leadership # 2

Empathy

- Did I see a situation from a team member's **perspective**?

- Did I regularly ask team members "**How are you doing**?"

- Did I **actively listen**, be truly **present** in a conversation
  with a team member?

Daryl D. Black

www.daryldblack.com

EMPATHY AND ITS IMPORTANCE TO LEADERSHIP

As a kid, do you remember doing something wrong and your parents getting upset at you? Let's say for example, that you hit another kid on the playground, but it was after that kid pushed you down. The supervisor didn't see the first part of the altercation but sure as heck saw you throw a punch. Your parents are called and instead of hearing your side of the story, they grounded you. Your side didn't matter.

What about at work when you've been working longer hours than normal to meet a tight deadline? You've been a committed team member and then the decision is made to crunch the timeline even more. No one has considered the impact to your workload or your schedule.

Or you're new to a team and given a task that you clearly aren't familiar with, don't have the tools for or the knowledge to carry out? The manager doesn't recognize or acknowledge the tough position you've been put in.

None of these examples seem to be connected on the surface but in the context of empathy, they absolutely are.

ARENT EMPATHY AND SYMPATHY THE SAME THING?!

Before we continue, let's get this out of the way right here at the outset. Empathy is the ability to recognize and share the emotions of another person, in this case someone on the team you support.   It involves a situation from another person's perspective and in sharing the associated emotion. Sympathy is a feeling of care and concern for someone and often felt as feeling 'bad' for someone because we want to see them happier or suffering less. If nothing else, you've learned something new today. You're welcome ;-)

WHY DOES EMPATHY MATTER?

There is a lack of empathy in each example and this has created a negative emotion and barrier between the 'leader' and the individual. Think back to your own similar experiences. The message being heard is that you don't matter and the 'leader' is the authority. Phrases like, 'You need to be a good soldier" or "Suck it up, Buttercup" are often used outright. You get the idea. So, instead of the opportunity to grow a connection (and loyalty and respect) with the individuals, we distance ourselves from the very people we need to get tasks done. Will the tasks get done? Yeah, likely. Will this lack of empathy cost us in the long run? Absolutely.

SERVANT LEADERSHIP REQUIRES EMPATHY

The movement toward less 'leader-centric' leadership and more 'servant' leadership is accompanied and driven by the increased presence of empathy. If we are empathetic, or, to put it another way, in tune with how one of our team may see a situation or circumstance, we can make a stronger connection than if we didn't consider something aside from our own perspective. As a leader, this can be difficult because there is a tendency to turn inwards and view everything through the lens that best serves our individual needs. Don't worry, it's completely natural.

In the context of crisis, a huge factor is stress which basically invokes the famous 'fight or flight' response. The surrounding people are very likely feeling increased anxiety and most likely so are you. Resist the urge to think just about yourself and what YOU are feeling and needing. That isn't how you'll be the most effective. That's a hard lesson and one of the burdens of leadership.

THE TAKEAWAY

We need to put our team first. Put ourselves in their shoes. While seemingly counter-intuitive (your natural tendency will be to put your needs first), it is an effective and critical way to build connections with the individuals on your team.

CONFESSIONS OF A NON-EMPATHETIC LEADER– A PERSONAL ANECDOTE

A recent personal anecdote about empathy, more specifically the lack of it. The main character is yours truly and this is a failure on my part to demonstrate it effectively during an initial exchange with someone I supported. I am pleased to say this is a rare exchange but demonstrative of how quickly an opportunity could be lost to build a connection with a team member.

THE SITUATION

The backdrop is an emergency in northern Alberta. I needn't go into the specifics or background, but I was in a leadership position supporting some 40 or so individuals through a couple of deputies (think of managers). I was having a particularly hard day and it was only 8:00 in the morning. We were doing a high-profile plan for citizen re-entry and the team was cross functional/inter-disciplinary and had people from all over the province. I had just left a meeting; my cortisol levels were high (aka I was feeling anxious) and I barged into our planning room to remove an ad hoc hand scribbled sign from the wall (it was the name of the working group that was situated in the room) to have it more 'professionally' done. That's it. I took it off the wall and was walking out when someone from the back of the room stood up and said "Hey, what are you doing with our sign?"

The nature of the team was such that we had people rotating in and out on a very regular basis (a team-building challenge to discuss another time) and this individual had arrived late the previous afternoon, but I hadn't met him yet. I didn't know who he was, and he certainly didn't know me. His physical demeanor was such he was challenging me. I IMMEDIATELY dismissed him and started to walk out. He added, "No matter what you think, we need to be included in what's happening out there (meaning the emergency)." I furrowed my brow at him and said, "Don't worry about it" and stormed out. Yes, mature.

THE SUBCONSCIOUS KICKS IN

Here's where it gets really interesting. In that split second, in less than a blink of an eye, this is what went through my head:

- Who is THIS guy?
- WHO does he think he is?
- Doesn't he know who I am?!
- Doesn't he know that I'm in charge?
- Doesn't he know that I'm kind of a big deal?! (Okay, that didn't flash through but it may as well have).

As if that wasn't enough, I subconsciously assessed him further:

- He wasn't from my organization.
- He wasn't wearing a fancy uniform adjourned (adorned) with fancy crests.
- He was shorter than me (yes, you want me to be authentic!).

Just so we're clear. I didn't consciously go through this checklist to validate whether I should pay heed to him or what he was saying. This was in a split second. My subconscious employed a technique called 'Stonewalling' where we put up a psychological barrier between us and someone else. It is especially common when we can't physically separate ourselves (i.e. the 'flight' part of stress response) and like I said, it's subconscious.

I walked out of the room to get this sign done up properly and upon reflection, I quickly realized that it was not an exchange I was proud of. I returned to the room and he was already discussing the interaction with others from his agency in the hallway. It was likely along the lines of me being an arrogant prick. I apologized, explained that it was not consistent with my values and not how I want to treat people. He was upset. We shook hands and normally that's it. But it wasn't. He continued to express his displeasure post-handshake (the unwritten rule says that a handshake should be the end of it, I hasten to add) and by then, I had already determined I was wrong from the outset. Some of you are thinking that I should've stopped him and took control again. The young leader in me would've stopped him cold in his tracks. In fact, I wouldn't have even apologized. Truth be known, I wouldn't have even recognized ANY issue. Fortunately, we landed on a great resolution and he became a great advocate and ally.

EMPATHY IN ACTION

So why didn't I shut him down? The answer lies in empathy. From the millisecond I walked into that room, I was only thinking about myself. I didn't acknowledge anyone. I was pissed off at something completely outside of the team's control. It was all about ME. I was going to fix something. I was going to make something right. I was only worried about my own thoughts and emotions. Then, when the team member stood up and 'challenged' me, I went deeper into myself and it manifested poorly. I met his challenge with greater challenge and shut him down. I shut him down because in that brief moment, I made it about ME. I was the LEADER and he was the follower. I was in charge. I had the authority. I was a big deal, he wasn't. He was experiencing more stress than me as he was COMPLETELY out of his element. I had at least been part of large operations before. Of course, he would be protective and in survival mode. And abrasive. I didn't think of that at the time.

I recounted this story to someone a while later and she looked at me and said: "Um, I don't get it. You took that situation pretty hard. He's lucky you even talked to him after that." Right then and there I thought to myself: this person doesn't get it.

THE TAKEAWAY

Empathy is SO critical. This had nothing to do with a sign. It had everything to do with ignoring a basic tenet of leadership: connect with the individuals. Put yourself in their shoes. Understand THEIR perspective. Lesson learned.

"One of the hallmarks of effective leadership is empathy. It means the ability to understand something from someone else's point of view. I am advocating more empathy, more servant leadership where the leader is a facilitator rather than the only driver of progress."

Daryl D. Black

@daryldblack

PILLAR #3: COMPASSION

- Did I beat myself up for a decision or action taken?

- Did I show kindness to a team member? Or myself?

- Did I support a team member who made a mistake?

The 1:100 Leadership Solution

Personal Pillar of Effective Leadership # 3

Compassion

- Did I beat myself up for a decision or action taken?

- Did I show kindness to a team member? Or myself?

- Did I support a team member that made a 'mistake'?

BE COMPASSIONATE TO CONNECT WITH YOUR TEAM

Another behaviour that builds connection is demonstrating compassion. The hard charging leader is a paradigm that needs to change. In order to connect with the individuals on the team, it is important to demonstrate that you genuinely care about their well-being. One of the ways is by amping up our level of compassion. To define what compassion is, an effective way is to list similar words: pity, sympathy, feeling, fellow feeling, empathy, understanding, care, concern, solicitude, solicitousness, sensitivity, tender-heartedness, soft-heartedness, warm-heartedness, warmth, love, brotherly love, tenderness, gentleness, mercy, mercifulness, leniency, lenience, tolerance, consideration, kindness, humanity.

Some questions to ask yourself about compassion:

- Did I stop beating myself up for a decision or action taken?
- Did I show kindness to a team member?
- Did I support a team member who made a mistake?

DONT OVERDO IT

Like all leadership concepts, it is about balance. If you are TOO compassionate, then you will be a pushover. You will also subjugate the vision and be very unpredictable when dealing with individuals because you will be over-responding to every single want they have.

If the team sees and KNOWS that you care about their well-being, they will be more respectful toward you and will align far more easily with where you need the team to go.

The following quote was first put on my radar by one of my favourite speakers of all time, Brene Brown (*Daring Greatly* and other books, TED Talk), and really encapsulates the journey that is leadership and working toward the solution to a problem. It rings as true today as it did when President Roosevelt gave this speech in 1910.

MAN IN THE ARENA

"It is not the critic who counts; not the man who points out how the strong man stumbles, or where the doer of deeds could have done them better. The credit belongs to the man who is actually in the arena, whose face is marred by dust and sweat and blood; who strives valiantly; who errs, who comes short again and again, because there is no effort without error and shortcoming; but who does actually strive to do the deeds; who knows great enthusiasms, the great devotions; who spends himself in a worthy cause; who at the best knows in the end the triumph of high achievement, and who at the worst, if he fails, at least fails while daring greatly, so that his place shall never be with those cold and timid souls who neither know victory nor defeat."

YOU DONT HAVE TO BE PERFECT – COMPASSION

As I write this, I'm reflecting back on those thousands of people who have experienced crisis in their lives. For example, the Ft. McMurray Wildfire. To date one of the largest wildfires in the world and Canada's costliest disaster, it decimated a community, forcing the emergent evacuation of some 88,000 residents. The wildfire destroyed 1,595 buildings in a very short time. It was nicknamed 'The Beast.' Pictures of residents driving perilously close to flames 100 feet tall were all over the Internet. No Photoshop needed. I have the perspective from being a member of an amazing team that responded following the fire working out of the Regional Emergency Ops Centre. This type of event is happening throughout the world, so the following words apply everywhere.

Also, I recently met with a dear friend of mine who experienced a loss due to a tragic accident. I met his wife and daughter as well. A poignant comment was made that he and his family is taking it hour by hour, not day by day. This is a sentiment shared by evacuees, families dealing with a tragic loss, people going through their own crisis.

The struggle to make sense of a tragedy, to put the chaotic emotions into some sort of order, is real. It's natural. But the process is wrought with frustration and judgment. The judgment doesn't just come from the outside although that's common: "You need to (insert advice here)." Worse, far more insidious is the judgment that comes from WITHIN. The need to figure things out without a manual. The need to get through the pain to the point where you can at least put together a full day without bowing out of a phone conversation or being able to leave the house.

To all of you feeling the chaos that crisis brings, the people who lost their homes, the first responders, to my dear friend and his family, everyone trying to navigate through any difficult situation, I say this:

We don't have to have all the answers. Give ourselves a pass. Forgive yourself for not having a clear path. If you're a leader, forgive yourself for not having a pain-free and well-defined path for your team or family. For not having the silver bullet to take all the pain away. The pain felt by those who you love and take care of.

Crisis strikes us all, and it strikes us all in different ways. We each have our filters by which we see a situation. By the very nature of crisis, there are no clear answers. Information is lacking, time is a factor and stress levels are high and that perpetuates the crisis. There are no easy answers. Cognitively, it's easy to think that time will heal everything; that the worst is over. But viscerally you don't believe it. This causes further misalignment. The cycle continues.

During this crisis, have you treated others with less respect than you normally would during this really difficult time? Possibly. Have you 'failed' to live up to this Herculean role as the 'leader' of your tribe (family, team, organization)? Likely. Have you felt lost, rudderless? Uh-huh. Have you detached and become withdrawn instead of leaning in and engaging? Yeah, at times I'm sure that's the case.

The fact that I have definitely hit on one or two behaviours should be a clear lesson for you. Those reactions are natural. Those are very common. It means you give a shit, and that's good. You care about your tribe. You care about the outcome. But when you care, you hurt more.

My advice is this: Be kind to yourself, particularly as you reflect on the past year if you're an evacuee or a first responder. Or reflecting on the past six weeks if you've suffered a tremendously painful loss like my friend and family has. Keep the self-judgment to a minimum. This is a journey that requires you to rely heavily on your intuition, your gut. You must determine what it'll take to get through this. No one else can tell you that. You need to look inward and feel what's right because your cognition isn't where the path will be revealed. Lean on others for support too.

THE TAKEAWAY

But forgive yourself. And keep forgiving yourself for not being 'perfect.' You're doing the best you can. And that's all anyone can ask of another and more importantly - themselves.

"Today, as a Leader, be **compassionate**.

Compassionate to **others** and
most importantly **yourself**."

Daryl D. Black

www.daryldblack.com

PILLAR #4: PERSONAL STRESS MANAGEMENT:

- Did I recognize moments of self-stress? When and why?
- Did I take steps to mitigate my stress proactively?

- Did I recognize self-stress and act accordingly to deal with it?

The 1:100 Leadership Solution

Personal Pillar of Effective Leadership # 4

1. Personal Stress Management

- Did I recognize moments of self-stress?
  When and why?

- Did I take steps to mitigate my stress proactively?

- Did I recognize self-stress and act accordingly
  to deal with it?

Daryl D. Black

www.daryldblack.com

PERSONAL STRESS MANAGEMENT– BUT WE DONT HAVE SABRE –TOOTHED TIGERS ANYMORE

Along with three very important internal pillars to leadership- vulnerability, empathy, compassion- there is a fourth. This is one that is particularly important because it is insidious in its nature if not understood and in fact leveraged. That pillar is stress. So much has been said and written about stress over the years and this is not the forum by which to deep dive into the neurological processes. I'm not an 'ologist' remember?! I have studied stress for many years in both theoretical and practical forums and a very basic understanding is in order. It is a series of reactions to a threat. Chemicals get dumped into our system that basically provide for a 'fight or flight' response (blood to muscle groups, some systems given lower priority like immune or digestive, elevated heart rate).

CEO AND CAVEPERSON

Mentally there are changes as well. There is a CEO in our brain. The CEO is the one responsible for complex thoughts, being able to determine cause and effects, handle complicated equations and work through issues to find solutions. There is also an associated Caveperson working in another part of our brain. The Caveperson has been around a long time and is responsible for the nuts and bolts operation of the body and while extremely capable at certain things, this poor Caveperson isn't well-equipped to calculate the square root of 64. Ask the Caveperson to get us out of trouble when confronted with a sabre-toothed tiger? Done. Figure out the complexity of human being interaction at a deeper level or make decisions with a lot of variables? The CEO is who you need to look to. Both have their place, and both are critical.

WE ACTUALLY NEED STRESS

It's a misnomer that all stress is bad. We actually NEED stress to perform at optimal levels. If an athlete is told unequivocally that they are on a team, then during tryouts their effort and performance will likely be less than perfect. Tell that athlete that they need to step it up and then the performance should rise accordingly.

SHOULD being the key word. Under high levels of stress, here's essentially what happens. The CEO recognizes that there is a lot of stress and packs up his briefcase and leaves his brain office to head to the cottage for the weekend. The CEO isn't needed because the ability to calculate causal effects, navigate through myriad variables and strategic thinking isn't important in a confrontation with a sabre-tooth tiger. Before the CEO leaves, they shout at the Caveperson using small words, saying something like: "Hey buddy, you don't need me. We're in survival mode and that's where you come in. Keep us alive, deal with the threat and I'll come back." Caveperson grunts and gets back to pumping chemicals into our system and preparing for the 'battle' to come.

Now you're thinking that there are no longer sabre-tooth tigers around and I'm not a zoologist but I think you're right. Yet we still experience stress. Why? Simply, the threat over the years has changed but our REACTION to it has not.

Later, I'll talk about why that has dire consequences and why it is so important for leaders to recognize stress, its impacts and have real strategies to deal with it in themselves and the teams they support.

THE TAKEAWAY

Start paying attention to what happens to your thinking and communication when you experience stress. That's a huge first step.

PERSONAL STRESS AND ITS DANGEROUS EFFECT ON LEADERSHIP

Why is it that we don't make the right decisions all the time when we're under stress? How do we miss seemingly hugely obvious pieces of the puzzle?

We've talked about stress, the CEO and Caveperson and why we actually need stress or a form of it to perform at optimal levels. Remember when we said that the CEO leaves the Caveperson in charge? That's well and good if the threat or challenge requires a response more physical (speed, strength etc.). The problem is that today very few of our stressors are physical in nature. We don't have to hunt, generally we don't have to have a life or death battle each day to return to our families (exception being combat, and I salute all those who serve). Our 'threats' are now things like financial, relationship, professional. The threat has changed but our reaction to it has not! The threats are even more complex and not as easily solved in the complexities of society and interpersonal relationships. This is a critical point when we talk about stress.

The body puts the Caveperson in charge and we've established that the Caveperson is ill-equipped to handle any type of complexity or higher thought. Examples of stress reactions we may experience are tunnel vision (to focus on the immediate threat at hand) which in turn cuts us off from hearing everything, irritability (subconscious struggles to gain control) which makes us less approachable by others, shutting down (subconscious determining that enough is enough) so we disengage instead of leaning in to solve a problem, unconscious use of Doomsday thinking (there is a time and place for this worst-case scenario thinking by the way). Longer term impacts include illness (our immune system isn't needed in a battle with a sabre-tooth tiger) and digestive problems (digesting food can wait), increased uses of substances like alcohol or drugs (trying to dampen or dull the feelings) …the list goes on.

From a personal perspective, we need to recognize that our words, actions, behaviours all impact the team. We are responsible for setting the tone, for providing mentorship, making decisions and supporting the team. Under personal stress, there is a real and tangible impact in that we will be more withdrawn, our behaviour changes and our ability to take in and process information is greatly deteriorated. If we are irritable, then it will heighten the team's stress because our leadership attitude is contagious. The team members may be reluctant to approach you with issues. If we need to think strategically, then stress is detrimental because we may have tunnel vision and our solutions won't take everything into account (and remember when we snapped at a team member? They aren't going to give you bad news and at least will soften it).

THE TAKEAWAY

Pay attention to stress reactions of yourself and others. Deliberately and consciously think about how that affects your decision-making and ability to make the right decisions. How stress leads to impatience.

"Today, as a Leader, **manage your stress**.

Figure out your **triggers**.
Take a **deep breath**.
Disengage to gather your thoughts."

Daryl D. Black

www.daryldblack.com

KNOW YOURSELF–

A TOOL TO MAKE YOU RECOGNIZE YOUR PERSONAL STRESSORS AND REACTIONS

We've talked about stress and why it is such an impairment for us, especially as problems become more complex and the variables seemingly infinite. Examples include:

-    Causing us to withdraw (disengagement creates distance between leader and the team);
- To become less compassionate (it becomes about 'you' and not the team);
-    Complex decisions are more difficult to make (remember our CEO is no longer in charge).

Remember, these are just examples. Stress is a highly complex series of reactions and these reactions are specific to the individual.

In an effort to make this into something practical, here is a self-assessment for you relating to your own stress and your reactions. There are general patterns of behaviour but ultimately, stress is something each of us experiences differently and at different thresholds.

Self-awareness is SO important and under stress we need to be very aware of how we are impacting others. Stress is a really quick and insidious way to undermine your relationship with your team and create tension. As leaders, one of our main goals is to create connection with the individuals on the team we support. Unmitigated stress can destroy that connection in a heartbeat.

KNOW YOURSELF ASSESSMENT

You can download a full-sized version at
www.daryldblack.com

1. What are your most common stress reactions?

- o   Irritability
- o   Shut down
- o   Physically removing yourself from the situation
- o   Being aggressive
- o   Inability to relax
- o   Increased use of humour (often inappropriate)
- o   Denial
- o   Other?_____________________________________

____

2. Think back to the last time you experienced this stress reaction. What circumstances, situation or conditions triggered it?

____

____

How would anyone around you know that you are experiencing stress?
You are:

- o   Being 'short' and terse with others
- o   Micro-managing
- o   Fidgeting/restless
- o   Speaking quickly
- o   Being forceful in your approach
- o   Not engaging in dialogue
- o   Other?_______________________________

____

3. Once you recognize you are experiencing stress what SPECIFICALLY could you do to mitigate it?

- o   Focus on one issue at a time
- o   Ask for help
- o   Take a deep breath and re-focus
- o   Remove yourself temporarily from the situation
- o   Take a break
- o   Other?____________________________________

____

4. When OTHERS recognize your stress reactions what do you want them to do?

- o Give you a verbal cue:

  ____

  ____

- o Take you aside and ask how they can help
- o Bring some appropriate humour to you
- o Tell you that you need a break and they've 'got this'
- o Other?_____________________________

  ____

MY OWN STRESS REACTIONS AND MITIGATION

For me, three stress reactions come to mind. They are rapid speaking, irritability and need to micromanage.

SO AMAZING AT COMMUNICATING POORLY

I always talk to process my thoughts. This is okay when my thoughts are coherent and specific. During crisis, this is not always the case, so I tend to do an amazing job of communicating poorly. I spout off a run-on sentence that often contradicts itself and leaves the receiver a bit baffled and rightfully so. To mitigate this, I ask the receiver to re-state what they think I said. It's a great technique to act as a checkpoint and allows me to hear what was heard. This is often different than what I intended. So powerful, easy to do and extremely beneficial to minimize tension and mistakes.

IRRITABILITY

As far as irritability, I strive to remove myself from the situation and take a DEEP, deliberate breath. It's amazing how good it feels and sometimes it literally feels like I haven't taken a breath all day!

NEED TO MICRO-MANAGE

For micro-management, I first recognize that the higher the profile or 'stakes', the more my desire to want to meddle. This is exactly the OPPOSITE of what a leader should do. I'll have created a culture of empowerment and delegation but then when things are really hectic or high profile, I jeopardize that and look over everyone's shoulder. To mitigate this, I first know that it is a tendency. I also ask and EXPECT my team to let me know with a simple phrase: "Daryl, I got this." It's even accompanied by a 'hand' gesture! You know what? Instead of being offended, I am very glad to have that. It's a respectful, pre-arranged signal. To be clear, everyone on the team knows it's my prerogative as the leader to go where I need to do, ask probing questions and manage the process. I try to avoid that as much as possible because the people I support are there for a reason.

Remember, this is about the team and the overall results. As a leader, we need to recognize when we are actually impeding our team's ability to perform at a high level. Unmitigated stress is one sure-fire way to kill teamwork and raise tension among the team.

THE TAKEAWAY:

Complete the assessment and discuss with your team. This is important. Trust me.

STRESS MANAGEMENT 101– IRRITABILITY: THINGS YOU CAN DO TO HANDLE IT

Irritability is a very common stress reaction and worthy of further discussion. I offer this as an example of recognizing stressors and stress reactions in the hopes it may be like yours or tweak something to lead you to a discovery.

STRESSOR: UNNECESSARY NOISE

I dislike a really noisy incident command post, emergency operations centre or workspace. Correction: I dislike an unnecessarily noisy incident command post, emergency operations centre or workspace. Noise is inherent in these environments and often indicates activity, discussions, solutions being found, information gathered. A hockey dressing room is loud. I'm okay with that. A concert is loud. A conference floor is noisy. Understood. Noise is a very healthy and necessary part of a work environment that is effective.

So why is this a stressor if I know this is normal?! Notice the word 'unnecessarily.' What's interesting is that it isn't my conscious mind that makes that determination. I have a low tolerance for noise that is unnecessary. That means that if I'm in Emergency Ops Centre (a room, or series of rooms where emergency management works), and I hear loud conversations not pertaining to the issues at hand I get irritated. If that same volume of conversation is happening but there is a solution being worked out, then I'm okay with it.

SUBCONSCIOUS ROLE IN FILTERING

I'm not consciously listening to every conversation happening in the room, but rest assured, my subconscious is constantly scanning visually and taking in auditory cues. It's filtering them so as to not overwhelm the conscious mind. An example would be at a party and you're talking to someone and then from another part of the party, you hear your name.

The concept of multi-tasking is a misnomer and will be discussed in another section. To be able to work through a myriad of factors we need to focus. Excessive noise means that our subconscious is needing to expend resources on scanning and analyzing our environment constantly and it is exhausting. But if the noise is related to what we're trying to solve, then the noise is deemed 'necessary' and therefore 'okay.' That doesn't mean that a really loud room is comfortable. It just means I have more tolerance.

MITIGATION

1. Be Proactive
To mitigate this, first I recognize the conditions in which my stress will rise. I can be proactive (set up in another space, create some ground rules where we talk in normal tones and not the excited loudness that can accompany others in stressful states) AHEAD of time in anticipation of a chaotic environment.

2. Discuss with the Team- They Can Help!
As well, I will have had the stress reaction discussion with my entire team or at least some from the team so they can see that I'm becoming irritated and either change some variables of the environment and/or let me know in a constructive and pre-determined way. One way is to ask me if I'm okay with a knowing look or subtle wink…that's a cue and a good one.

3. Re-Statement

When I get irritable, I also 'communicate' in shorter sentences and tend to be more sarcastic. By asking someone to re-state (or have the expectation that when important information is exchanged, or tasks given that the receiver automatically restates), I can see how ineffective I'm being at conveying my thoughts. That is often a wake-up call for me to take a deep breath and de-stress somehow.

This is one example of a stress reaction, why it is such and what myself and the team does to help me through it.

THE TAKEAWAY

Work through the Personal Stress Assessment.

STRESS MANAGEMENT 101– MICROMANAGEMENT: THE PROLIFIC STRESS REACTION & WHAT YOU CAN DO ABOUT IT!

We've discussed the nature of stress and stress reactions. A very common stress reaction, some would argue a prolific one at that, is the behaviour of micromanagement. Detail-oriented. Involved. Hands on. If you or your boss has ever used words like that to describe your management style, then there is a chance that you demonstrate behaviours of a micro-manager. In addition to irritability, micromanagement is another one of my stress reactions so let's explore it further.

STRESSOR: PERCEIVED LACK OF CONTROL

Stress builds at the fear of the unknown. In the context of crisis, there are A LOT of unknowns. If the situation is personal crisis, then it's where will the money come from? How will the kids react? What if I can't find anyone else to share a life with? Who will I turn to for help? On the professional side, unknowns include will I have a job? Who will I report to? Will I need to take less money to keep my job? The unknowns are virtually infinite.

Circling back to why the unknown is such a stressor is because in the Caveperson days, uncertainty meant death and suffering. If my Cave ancestors were eternal optimists, then I wouldn't be here banging away on this keyboard. Unknowns to the Caveperson were a direct threat to their well-being and that of the Cave family. Take that into the modern context. When we started to form communities, then unknowns were treated with equal disdain because certainty means we know where our food is coming from, we know where we fit in the hierarchical system in which we govern ourselves. Unknowns meant suffering. Knowns represented control.

WHY IS MICROMANAGEMENT SO COMMON?

Micromanagement happens when we don't think we have control over a situation (crisis is filled with challenges to control). It is particularly relevant when there is something high profile or particularly high stakes. Our 'NEED' to control the outcome skyrockets. To essentially KNOW how things will turn out means less stress and more comfort. If it's insignificant, then we often don't care about the outcome, so we don't worry about it and therefore don't micromanage. It's easy to be hands-off when we don't actually care about the outcome.

MY OWN EXPERIENCE

During crisis, there are more unknowns than knowns. If my personal relationships aren't solid, then there is an innate desire to deep dive into that. If I am in an emergency operations centre (an emergency response HQ), then it is absolutely staggering how my need to get more 'hands-on' gets. Briefing to a senior government official? Then I WANT to pay attention to the type of font on the graphs. I kid you not. Sans serif vs Times New Roman. The debate continues. I know that as sure as I know that it will get dark at night. The higher the stakes, the more my need to try to control the outcome. What do I do when I need to control the outcome? I pay a visit to everyone on the team…and then I visit them again. I have a desire to reinforce how important X project is. Yeah, as if they need that. They aren't stupid. That's why they are on the team.

When I micromanage, I am essentially telling them that I don't trust them to do a good job. Think about that. It's not my intention at all. But it's what they see. Think hard about that again. It's important. Also, when I micromanage them, then THEY are micro-managing those that they support. It goes downhill.

As discussed, one of the most critical components to stress management is to recognize the stressor and our reactions to it. The above speaks to this in a nutshell. So, I know the problem but how do I go about minimizing my need to micromanage?

MITIGATION

1. Be Proactive:
Recognize the conditions in which you'll want to micromanage. In other words, know when you feel the stakes are high.. Recognize what you know is or will be important. You'll notice that the higher the profile or the more important you think something is, the more you'll want to get 'detail-oriented.'

2. Discuss with the Team- They Can Help!
I have this discussion with every team I support. Remember that as the leader, I am there for them not vice versa. Some of the crises I'm a part of have tremendously significant consequences in terms of life, human suffering and economic impact (being in the HQ for Canada's two largest natural disasters for example). So, I make sure that the team knows that it is my temptation and that I need their help. I can be VULNERABLE with them.

3. The 'Signal'
From there, I ask them to give me a quick signal: an open hand and the words: "Daryl, I got this." That is such an effective technique because it is respectful, clear and concise.

Just so I'm crystal clear, the team knows that I reserve the right to deep dive whenever and wherever I want. My position grants me that so I am not giving anything up. No authority is relinquished. I am ultimately responsible for the outcome and everyone knows that.

THE TAKEAWAY

Do your Personal Stress Assessment. It's important.

"As a Leader, the good news and bad news is that your **attitude** and **outlook** is contagious.

Choose your words and actions deliberately."

Daryl D. Black

www.daryldblack.com

ADDITIONAL GUIDANCE

LEADERS: BORN OR MADE?

I hear the phrases, 'he's a born leader', 'he's a natural leader', 'born to lead' (more on the gender bias later) a lot. You used those phrases when we met last actually. The phrases evoke an image of one who captures a crowd with their speech. "People follow them without hesitation, a brilliant orator, one who exudes charisma, confidence."

The inverse is also true. "They are a tyrant." Or "A micro-manager." Do you really think that those 'poor' leaders are BORN with those traits?

Leaders: born or made?

"Leadership is a set of skills and behaviours; skills and behaviours can be learned through dedication, obtaining knowledge, practice, feedback and refinement."

Daryl D. Black

@daryldblack

PRACTICE MAKES PERFECT

Let's look at it another way, a more objective and realistic way I'd submit. We should say this person exhibits a number of behaviours and traits that make people choose to follow. They have the skills that build respect in their followers, an ability to communicate well, make decisions and nurture trust among the team and others. This individual, through various means, effectively provides purpose, direction and motivation to others. There is a popular book written by Malcolm Gladwell called "The Outliers?" In it, Gladwell writes about the '10,000' hour rule. Basically, to be an expert at something, you need to put in 10,000 hours of practice. It's received a lot of attention and has become the de facto 'standard'. Of course, there has been some debate about the scientific or behavioral validity of that statement but I think we can all agree with the fact that practice makes perfect. A mantra I use is, don't practice until we get it right. Practice something until we don't get it wrong.

THE GREAT ONE

Let's talk about the Great One, Wayne Gretzky. He is revered as being one of the greatest hockey players in history. His point totals are staggering, and he holds a huge number of records. He was a child prodigy by all accounts. He had a natural talent for hockey. What is missed in all the discussions about The Great One is the fact that in the winter, before school each and every morning, Gretzky was outside on the homemade rink his dad, Walter, made in the backyard. After school, Gretzky would put his skates back on and back to the rink he went. In addition, he played on several teams as well. In the spring and summer months, Gretzky played baseball. That sport promotes eye/hand coordination, something extremely important when you are trying to receive a pass while moving quickly on a part of your stick that is 3-4 feet from your hands. Oh, and do it while watching for other players because missing something in that environment would result in suffering a painful hit. Simply put, he worked extremely hard and very deliberately on the skills of hockey.

Further, how did he know what he needed to work on? His father, Walter, was at every game, every practice and provided feedback. Gretzky had metrics as well in the form of points (goals, assists and others) by which he could determine his progress. A quote attributed to Gretzky was that instead of being where the puck was, he always went where the puck was going to be."

Let's look at it another way, from a neurological perspective. Through exhaustive repetition, deliberate review and analysis, Gretzky's subconscious was able to determine patterns and cues more rapidly than most others.

To imply that someone is born with everything they need to lead is not only incorrect, but it also ignores the fact that this person, either deliberately or through subconscious behavioural modeling, has learned the behaviours and obtained the skills over a period of time. It ignores the fact that if the leadership journey was undertaken on purpose through self-reflection, feedback and practice, the leader has had to work hard to get to where they are. It also ignores that leadership is not static. The leadership environment, the things that make up the circumstances, is constantly changing. It evolves and adapts depending on the audience. The followers.

Let's not forget that 'bad' leaders learned those behaviours so why don't you choose to learn how to be a GREAT leader?

It may take hard work, but we can all learn to be leaders and by extension, learn to be even better leaders if we already are good ones.

This list is no means exhaustive, but it will provide a framework. What are the skills or traits a leader needs to provide purpose, direction and motivation?
- Demonstrate emotional intelligence.
- Be a good communicator.
- Build and promote trust among the team.

- Able to make timely decisions.
- Have a vision and be able to articulate it.
- Hold themselves and others accountable.
- Know what makes each team member 'tick'.

So, what makes those things so difficult during crisis? Why is it that we tend to have such a hard time with those things when the chips are down, and the stakes are high?

Time is such a big factor, or lack of it in many cases. Everything seems to be urgent. The pace is so much quicker than it was before the crisis. We're constantly putting out fires (no pun intended) from everywhere, more than usual. Everyone is afraid to make a decision for fear of causing even more damage. Making a mistake. They're paralyzed and looking to their bosses for help who eventually continue to look upward. We have people scrambling to keep their jobs so they're working lots of overtime but not really sure where they fit in. How are they contributing to the bigger picture? These are symptoms of a larger issue that we'll talk about in the future.

It is so hard to make decisions, at least the right ones. Information is almost impossible to come by and when we do have it, it's usually wrong or conflicting. Often, some of our people have been elevated to positions that they aren't comfortable in and the responsibility and pressure is hugely uncomfortable for them. "I'm just not cut out for this," they say.

Let's take the 'Be a good communicator' characteristic. Communication in its simplest form involves a sender, a message, a receiver, and feedback. A critical skill that a leader needs is that of a good listener. They must be able to hear what someone is saying as opposed to just thinking of the next thing to say while the team member is talking. The ability to effectively listen builds a rapport through respect. The Boss is ACTUALLY listening to me, allows a chance for the leader to receive information and so on. So, can someone learn to not talk while another is talking? Of course. Can a leader learn to restate what the team member has just said? What I'm hearing you say is this? Basically, learn to shut the Hell up while someone is talking. Absolutely. That is just one example.

Another issue with anointing someone a 'born leader' is that the individual may be less likely to continue to seek improvement and become complacent. They will no longer elicit feedback and may make the step from confident to arrogant. They will fall victim to cognitive biases like 'Overconfidence' (we don't need a Plan B because Plan A will work) or 'Confirmation' (once I decide something, then everything I see will support my view). This will impede their growth as a leader and have a very adverse effect on the team.

Effective leadership is a set of behaviours and SKILLS, and like any behaviour or skill, it can be learned with practice. Now let's be clear. In athletics and business for example, there are those that have a seemingly natural affinity to pick something up quickly while others struggle. Of course. That said, all of us can learn something new and if we are dedicated and have the tools and guidance to obtain those skills, we can improve as a leader.

LETTERS AREN'T LEADERSHIP

I recently had a great conversation about leadership and the topic of position and credentials came up as these relate to leadership. Just because you have a certain position in the organization, on the team or formal credentials behind your name doesn't mean you are automatically a leader. Some examples that immediately come to mind are MBA, PhD, P.Eng, M.D., PCP, EMT, CA, CMA, AEIOU and sometimes Y. This applies to titles like CEO, COO, CFO, Director, Manager, Team Lead…You get the idea.

In my experience, leadership has little to do with the formal job title or formal credentials.

I'd submit to you that designations have nothing to do with being an effective leader. The danger for those who do possess said letters is that there is an assumption made within themselves that they have the position and the designation so they don't have to 'prove' that they're a leader or work at it. Nothing could be farther from the truth. Leadership is difficult. We are dealing with the most complex of variables: the human being. Personalities, attitudes, circumstances all mix together and it is the leader that must channel the group's strengths and weaknesses and move toward a common goal. This is done through connecting with the individuals on the team.

CREDENTIALS HAVE THEIR PLACE

I am not saying that credentials aren't important because they are. They denote a certain level of education, training, experience, etc. It differentiates some professionals from amateurs. They represent a standard being met. That is very important. All the above means an individual has demonstrated expertise and commitment in a particular field.

Note that while there are often leadership modules or lessons within those learning paths, leadership itself is extremely difficult to teach in a classroom setting. Leadership requires OJT (on-the-job-training) like few other endeavours. Only by being in the trenches, by trying to connect with the individuals, by evaluating and pivoting your approach numerous times can you begin to understand the intricacies, art and science behind effective leadership.

PRICE OF ARROGANCE

Often, there is an arrogance shown that because one has reached the pinnacle of a chosen profession that the 'soft' skills of leadership are naturally obtained. There is a caution to be had in that. Arrogance and a sense that you are the smartest person in the room are the foundation for:

- Team dysfunction;
- A large gap between the team and the leader;
- A team afraid to make decisions and is therefore risk-averse to the detriment of the goal;
- A team that supports the leader to the bare minimum.

EXAMPLE: HEALTHCARE

An area of particular concern is in the health care field, both pre-hospital (those on the front lines like Paramedics and similar) and the hospital setting. Those environments are replete with official credentials, fancy crests, logos, formal training, a strong hierarchy and ego. To be clear, those are demanding areas and a strong sense of worth and confidence is not only nice to have, it is a necessity. Difficult decisions need to be made and made with time always being a factor.

Physicians and nurses, paramedics and EMTS/EMRs must work hand-in-hand in the best interest of a patient. THAT is the WHY within our healthcare system. Simple as that. These systems exist for the patient. Period. This 'why' is often forgotten in the day-to-day battles waged on the ambulance and in the hospitals. People leverage their position and education to move things forward. While well-intentioned, this leveraging comes at the cost of connection between the different levels of the team. Yes, the nurses will support the doctor. They will work hard and diligently. But that work will be IN SPITE of the doctor in some cases and will sometimes be at the bare minimum. The same would apply for an overbearing paramedic interacting with a 'subordinate' (the term often used to make sure everyone knows the pecking order) in a pre-hospital setting. The job gets done but at the cost of leader/team connection and long term success.

A DOMINATING LEADER IMPEDES LONG TERM SUCCESS

With a leader trying to dominate and oftentimes impose their will, the team's long-term success is virtually impossible to achieve. For an effective response to crisis, there needs to be strong connections between all members of the team and the team must know that the leader:

- Is actually there to support them;
- Has the overall 'why' very much at the forefront;

- Has the ability to be vulnerable, be compassionate, be empathetic and to manage their stress levels well.

The healthcare industry is just an example. The above can be applied to ANY industry or even family situation.

So, remember, letters aren't leadership. If you have the letters, be mindful of your behaviours and interactions. If you don't have the letters, then it means you can and should step up to lead anyway.

THE TAKEAWAY

Look at yourself and pay attention to whether or not you find yourself using your credentials and position to make things happen. If so, then this is an opportunity to reflect and improve your ability to connect with the team you support.

How a team interacts & communicates
with you as the leader is not a reflection
on them.

It is direct reflection on how you
interact and communicate with them.

Daryl D. Black

www.daryldblack.com

POWER PARADOX: THE ANTIDOTE FOR MICROMANAGEMENT

Have you ever wondered why you'd go through a brick wall for some leaders while not daring to take one step off the pavement for another and in some extreme cases undermine them? Why, in situations that are literally life and death do we follow someone despite a primal fear? If you are a leader, then ask yourself, do you have a 'loyal' team? A team that listens well, responds well and goes ABOVE and BEYOND what you've asked? If the answer is no, then there is an opportunity to reflect on your leadership style among the other concepts we've covered specific to vulnerability, empathy, compassion and personal stress management.

WHAT IS LEADERSHIP POWER

So, why would I make such a bold and seemingly odd statement that if I give someone else 'power', then mine would actually INCREASE? Let's look at what I mean by power first. In leadership terms, I'm talking about the ability to influence behaviours, drive toward outcomes and produce outstanding TEAM results. Remember, as leaders, our job is to support the team and give them what they need not vice versa. If there is a goal to be reached, the team will work harder, longer and will actually be HAPPIER if we use the paradox effectively. If you do have a team that responds well, then there is a high likelihood that you've effectively used the Power Paradox. If you don't know what it means, don't worry, I've got you covered. Tactically, it looks like delegation, empowerment, hands-off techniques. To be honest, anything not related to micromanagement. In simplest terms, it means this:

A leader gains more 'power' by giving it away. Yes, you read that right.

It sounds incredibly counter-intuitive, doesn't it? Hence the paradox. If I DON'T meddle, don't go 'hands-on', don't get really into the weeds, then my leadership will not only remain intact but will in actuality grow and grow to the reaches of the team that you don't even directly interact with. Let's open the hood and look at it some more.

WHY DOES THE POWER PARADOX WORK?

Think about what motivates people. The team members want to feel like:

- They matter.
- That what they're doing matters.
- They're contributing.
- They're being treated like an adult.

 By asking a team member to carry out a task, you are telling them that you:

- RESPECT them.
- TRUST them.
- LIKE them.

If you think I'm out to lunch on this, then let's flip this around. What happens when you don't think someone respects you? Or doesn't trust you? Or doesn't even like you? You certainly aren't going to give them the keys to the kingdom, are you? In a work environment, you'll do the minimum required for your position. Maybe you have a strong internal compass and will do more but I'd suggest that you won't go through a brick wall. Okay, hyperbole. Work with me.

YOU ARENT GIVING UP RESPONSIBILITY OR AUTHORITY

I'm not saying that you need to abdicate your role as leader. As the leader, you must ensure that the goals are being met. There are techniques for effective delegation, but one concept is to give the team the End State (what right looks like). The team will see the end zone and they will know where they're going AND when they get there. That's your control as a leader.

As leaders, we need to make connections with the individuals on our team and if you want to do that, then use the Power Paradox. Delegate effectively more frequently because this empowers the individuals and collectively the team. It demonstrates TRUST and RESPECT. You'll see that this will permeate down to the different levels of the team.

THE TAKEAWAY

Ask yourself when was the last time you delegated something to someone else or the entire team? If you can't remember then try it. It's counter-intuitive but it works.

FACILITATE, DONT DICTATE! THE LEADER AS A FACILITATOR:

The Field General…Hard Charger…leading from the front…Tower of Strength…those terms conjure up mental images of what leadership is. You can almost 'feel' the tension and the battle raging. I'll let you in on a little secret though. That's what leadership WAS. Our leaders needed to be forces of nature where their sheer will was enough to win the day. Think about the World War II movies of beach storming where the leader stands up heroically, waves his hand in a grand gesture forward and yells out: "Forward!" Everyone leaps from behind their cover and rushes forward to confront the enemy. The armies throughout history were not defined by their accomplishments but more as being instruments of a single leader (insert General here): Napoleon, Patton, Rommel, Eisenhower etc.

Leaders were that way for a very good reason. They were highly involved in so many things because there wasn't technology to gather information, convey instruction or motivate teams. On a larger scale, there was great honour in working extremely hard and being hands-on as much as possible. Your accomplishments were measured by tangible results, whether it be the assembly of something or the covering of a map. We rewarded this with promotions and awards and for good reason.

Leaders **facilitate**,

they don't **dictate**

www.daryldblack.com

WHY LEADERSHIP NEEDS TO CHANGE

It's not what leadership is or should be today. Our teams are highly distributed among buildings, cities, countries and continents. The skillsets and personalities of the team members are as varied as the time zones in which the team operates. We simply can't be everywhere. We can't be all-knowing. We can't be on the front line anymore. If we insist on trying to be everywhere and control as much as possible, we are actually undermining the very team we support!

CRISIS LEADERSHIP ENVIRONMENT

In a crisis environment, the need for a different approach to leadership is even more acute. Events during crisis typically occur more quickly, are sometimes unexpected and our regular processes and team composition may not apply. And time…the precious element of time…may be in really short supply.

THE NEW LEADERSHIP LANDSCAPE

So, what does this mean to the current leadership landscape? It means that we must take on the role of facilitator. Another way is that of an orchestra composer. Instead of deep diving into each and every area and delivering instructions, we need to be an overseer.

OUR ROLE IN SETTING THE TEAM UP FOR SUCCESS

We must ensure that the team members are set up for success by (note, partial list):

- Recognizing our role is to SUPPORT the team, not the other way around;
- Connecting with as many individuals on the team as possible (through vulnerability, empathy, compassion and managing stress levels);
- Clearly defining team structures, roles and responsibilities (even if no formal documentation exists for this situation);
- Evaluating and ensuring that communication is occurring between team members, up and down as well;
- Communicating a clear End State (what right looks like);
- Establishing priorities;
- Equipping the team with the resources needed (tools, training, capacity).

FACILITATE, DONT DICTATE

Nowhere in this list is there the requirement to type for the team members, make decisions for the team members, tell the team members what to do and how to do it. Remember the Power Paradox? We gain power by giving it away. That is the premise for the leader as facilitator.

We definitely need to remain engaged, otherwise things will quickly spiral out of control without any direction. If we are facilitating effectively, the only things we'll have to figure out are problems beyond the ability of the team to handle in the form of escalations, removal of barriers or resourcing.

Remember that we are there to support the team and leave them to get the job done.

THE TAKEAWAY

Picture yourself as a composer in your next team conversation. No, don't grab a stick and stand on a chair. Do it mentally instead ;-)

MILLENNIALS ARENT THE PROBLEM. LABELS ARE

Ask yourself if you are the same as your sibling. Or look at other families and see if their kids are exactly the same. What about at work? Are you and your co-workers exactly the same even though you are roughly the same age? When you're in another country, is everyone from that country exactly the same? We all know the answers and that is a resounding no. Are there similarities? Of course. But there are differences too.

There has been a lot of attention lately around the 'Millennial' generation. Comparisons abound to 'Gen X', 'Gen Y (said Millennials)', Gen 'Z' and 'Baby Boomers'. Or different religions and political parties. What about the 'middle child' or anything else related to race, colour, religion and nationality? Or 'homeless' people? Turn on the news or check your Facebook newsfeed and you'll see headlines wrought with labels which are really nothing more than rhetoric and sweeping generalizations. While labels are effective at catching attention in a political speech or a news story, they actually undermine and erode effective leadership and our need to connect with individuals. Frankly the discussion around generations, religions and birth order (as examples) pisses me off.

WE ARENT ALL THE SAME

Heuristics

We like labels because they are heuristics, basically a rule of thumb or shortcut to avoid putting work on our cognitive brain. We can apply a label to something to make it more easily understood and digested which is why we see them in the media and during speeches for example. They resonate and don't require real effort to apply.

I've talked about the need to connect with those we support as leaders. Building trust is imperative and one of the ways is through vulnerability. Another critical way of bridging the gap between leader and follower is through learning to treat each member of our team as an INDIVIDUAL. There are really two overall reasons for this connection being so important and why the use of labels is counter-productive.

Micro-Level Impact

To bring out optimal performance and reduce stress, a team member needs to feel like they are valued. That they matter. That they're contributing in a meaningful way. One way is to ensure that you are finding out about them in a deeper way rather than using a label. They are wearing the same uniform (the classic uniform worn by emergency services, business suits, coveralls) but each of them is motivated differently, handles stress differently, processes information differently. I'm not suggesting that we do a long team-building session because during crisis, there simply isn't time. Take the time, whatever time you can to sit down and learn some basic things about each person. It shouldn't even be work-related. If we do that, then we will know what motivates them, what their personality is like, what makes them laugh and how they think.

Macro-Level Impact

Also, when we use labels, we are actually creating a barrier between teams as well. This barrier can be present from two people right up to a national level (country vs. country, West vs. East etc.). When I put on a uniform, I am saying that I belong to a particular team, a tribe. The worst thing I can do is now treat other tribes who are not wearing that same uniform as 'less than' or wildly different.

THE TAKEAWAY

There is SO much more than this to dive into. I'll leave you with this: Effective leadership is about building meaningful connections with those you support. Simply put, everyone you interact with is different. Ignore the uniform, ignore the job description, ignore their generational label, ignore where they're from. Build the relationship at the individual level and work upwards, NOT the other way around.

"One of the biggest mistakes a leader can make is assuming that because everyone on their team is wearing the same uniform, works for the same company or is labeled as a particular 'generation' that they're all the same. They aren't.

Connect with them as individuals first and always."

Daryl D. Black

@daryldblack

CONCLUSION

Congratulations! You are well on your way to being one who can first lead themselves and in turn lead others. You've learned that vulnerability isn't weakness, empathy is sorely needed and connects you so well with others, compassion is essential, particularly self-compassion. Finally, you now recognize that stress permeates so much of what we do and it really impedes our ability to relate and interact with others.

For more, be sure to check out:

daryldblack.com